This dragon book belongs to:

....

Train Your Dragon To Love Himself
My Dragon Books - Volume 13
Written by Steve Herman

ISBN: 978-1948040365 (paperback)
ISBN: 978-1948040372 (hardcover)

www.MyDragonBooks.com

First Edition: June 2018

10 9 8 7 6 5 4 3 2 1

Not many folks can say
they have a dragon of their own,
And with a dragon for a pal,
you'll never be alone.

A dragon is a loyal friend,
a very loving pet...

And with him by your side,
you're as safe as you can get!

Although my dragon loves me,
as anyone can tell...

Diggory had to learn
that he must love himself, as well.

Diggory has a tender heart,
although he's big and strong;

And I can always tell
whenever something's wrong.

"My snout is much too long," he said, as if his heart would crack – "What if my friends all laugh behind my back?"

"Diggory Doo," I told him,
"Your snout looks fine to me;
And I'm sure your friends
would certainly agree."

Soon Diggory Doo was sad again,
"What is it now?" I asked –
He said, "I ran a race at school,
but I'm not very fast."

"Although I did my very best,
another boy won."

"What difference does it make,"
I said, "how swiftly you can run?"

One day Diggory Doo just hung his head
and cried a little harder;
"Oh how I wish," he said,
"that I could be much smarter."

I told my dragon, "Diggory Doo,
I think you're smart enough,
And it's time you stop your crying
over unimportant stuff."

"You just don't understand," he said –
"Perhaps, you never will...
How it feels to be a dragon
with no talent and no skill."

"Diggory Doo," I said,
"I can't imagine why you're sad
When you're by far the coolest dragon
a kid has ever had!

"Now look into the mirror
and tell me what you see."

"Don't be silly," Diggory said.
"All I can see is me."

I told my dragon, "Look again!
Just take another peek;
See with your heart, and not your eyes,
what makes you so unique."

"So love the life you have;
be what you're meant to be;"

"Diggory, wipe your tears away
and hold your head up high,
For you don't need to feel ashamed;
you have no cause to cry."

"If you want to be the best,
then be the best at being YOU."

Diggory thought a moment, then said, "I think I see – Every life is special, including even me!"

Everyone is different,
but we all have love to give,
So show that love to others,
and love the life you live!

Get your FREE Gift from Diggory Doo at
www.MyDragonBooks.com/gift

Visit
www.MyDragonBooks.com
for more!